2

NATURE'S MYSTERIES

HOW B A T S
"SEE" IN THE DARK

Malcolm Penny

BENCHMARK BOOKS

MARSHALL CAVENDISH
NEW YORK

Benchmark Books
Marshall Cavendish Corporation
99 White Plains Road
Tarrytown, New York 10591-9001

Series created by The Creative Publishing Company

Library of Congress Cataloging-in-Publication Data
Penny, Malcolm.
　　　How bats see in the dark / Malcolm Penny.
　　　　　p.　　cm. -- (Nature's mysteries)
　　　Includes bibliographical references and index.
　　　Summary: Provides information about bats and, in particular, about
how they use their unique radar to find food and navigate in the air.
　　　ISBN 0-7614-0455-4 (lib. bdg.)
　　　1. Bats--Juvenile literature.　2. Echolocation (Physiology)-
-Juvenile literature.　[1. Bats.　2. Echolocation (Physiology)]
I. Title.　II. Series.
QL737.C5P36　1997
599.4--dc20　　　　　　　　　　　　　　　　　96-19940
　　　　　　　　　　　　　　　　　　　　　　CIP
　　　　　　　　　　　　　　　　　　　　　　AC

Printed and bound in the United States of America
Reprinted in 1998

Acknowledgments
Illustrated by Colin Newman
The publishers would like to thank the following for their permission to reproduce photographs: cover Stephen
Dalton/Oxford Scientific Films, title page Frank Greenaway/Bruce Coleman, verso Frank Greenaway/Bruce Coleman,
4 Stephen J. Krasemann/Bruce Coleman, 5 top Jose Luiz Gonzalez Grande/Bruce Coleman, 5 bottom Stephen
Dalton/Oxford Scientific Films, 6 John Neubauer/Bruce Coleman, 7 top Jane Burton/Bruce Coleman, 7 bottom Kim
Taylor/Bruce Coleman, 8 Frank Schneidermeyer/Oxford Scientific Films, 9 Frank Greenaway/Bruce Coleman, 11 Stephen
Dalton/Oxford Scientific Films, 12 Chris James/Bruce Coleman, 13 Frank Greenaway/Bruce Coleman, 15 Carol
Farneti/Partridge Films/Oxford Scientific Films, 16 Antonio Manzanares/Bruce Coleman, 17 Jens Rydell/Bruce Coleman,
18 top Kim Taylor/Bruce Coleman, 18 bottom Dave Roberts/Science Photo Library, 19 Kim Taylor/Bruce Coleman,
20 top Stephen Dalton/Oxford Scientific Films, 20 bottom Dieter & Mary Plage/Survival Anglia/Oxford Scientific Films,
21 Merlin D. Tuttle/Photo Researchers/Oxford Scientific Films, 22 top Kim Taylor/Bruce Coleman, 22 bottom Merlin D.
Tuttle/Photo Researchers/Oxford Scientific Films, 23 John Visser/Bruce Coleman, 25 Mark Deeble & Victoria
Stone/Oxford Scientific Films, 27 Klein Associates Inc./Science Photo Library, 28 Stephen J. Krasemann/Bruce Coleman,
29 top Merlin D. Tuttle/Photo Researchers/Oxford Scientific Films, 29 bottom Babs & Bert Wells/Oxford Scientific Films

(Cover) A greater horseshoe bat catches a moth.

CONTENTS

HOW BLIND IS A BAT?

Have you ever seen bats whizzing around chasing insects in near darkness on a summer evening? Have you wondered how they find their prey when there is little light to see by?

Bats can fly and find their food in complete darkness, but they do not use their eyes. We shall find out how skillful they are when hunting at night and how they do it — and how people discovered their secret.

Sometimes, we say that a person who cannot see very well is "blind as a bat." But bats aren't blind! They all have eyes, so they can at least tell light from darkness. Fruit-eating bats, in particular, can see very well.

People have always been amazed at the way bats can catch flying insects at night and fly among trees without crashing into them. Many live in caves, finding their roosting

At dusk, bats emerge from their daytime roosts to hunt for food. This gathering at Bracken Cave in Texas is the biggest in the world. Here, forty million Mexican free-tailed bats shelter during the day.

places and their babies in total darkness. More than two hundred years ago, scientists discovered that bats can do all these things if their eyes are covered but not if their ears are plugged. In 1938, a scientist at last found out how they use their ears. Their way of "seeing" in the dark is called echolocation.

▲ By roosting close together, bats keep warm in the often damp caves where they spend the day. These are greater horseshoe bats and Schreiber's bent-winged bats.

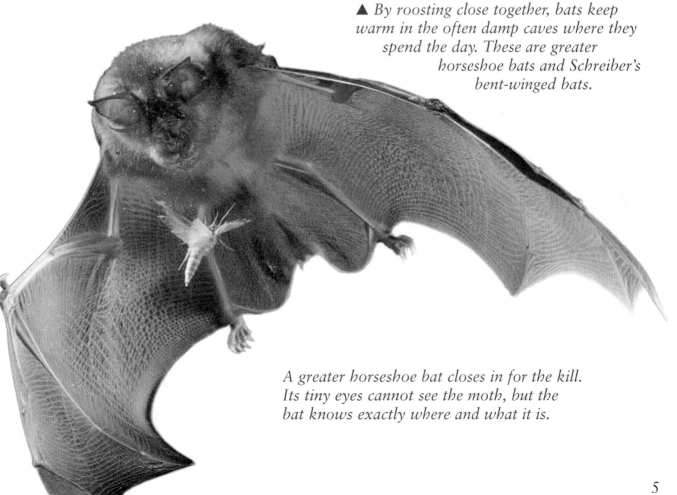

A greater horseshoe bat closes in for the kill. Its tiny eyes cannot see the moth, but the bat knows exactly where and what it is.

5

LISTEN TO THE WORLD

If you stand still with your eyes shut, you can get some idea of your surroundings by listening. Perhaps there is a river nearby or trees rustling in the wind. In a city, the noise of traffic or the crowd at a baseball game give clues about your surroundings. We can tell whether things are on our left or right because our brain can compare the sounds arriving at both our ears.

Most bats have large, external ears, often with complicated patterns of ridges and folds of skin. This shows that hearing is very important to them. Bats also have very large brains for their size. They use them to make sense of all the sounds they hear.

Bats listen to the world about them, just as people do. But they do much more than that: They make their own

You don't need eyes to know what is happening around you. The people on the riverbank in this scene are aware of many things at once: nearby conversations, the boat's engine and its passengers talking, water splashing, trees rustling, and the noise of traffic in the background.

sounds and listen for echoes coming back from objects nearby and far away. From these echoes, they can build up a picture of the world in sound.

Bats make some of these sounds in order to locate large objects such as branches and to find their way in caves. Other, different sounds enable them to find smaller things such as the insects they catch for food. How do they make these different sounds, and how do they use them?

▶ *The ridged ears of a long-eared bat with a separate flap in front help it tell where sounds are coming from.*

▼ *When it flies, the long-eared bat can avoid leaves and twigs in complete darkness.*

MAKING NOISES

Like humans and other vertebrates, bats make sounds by passing air through their voice box, or larynx. Some bats release the sound through their open mouths. Others use their noses, which may be even more complicated than their ears. You can often tell which bats these are by their names — leaf-nosed, slit-faced, or spear-nosed bats. The purpose of the different nose shapes is to focus the sound so that it comes out in a narrow beam like the light from a flashlight. As it flies, the bat turns its head from side to side, changing the shape of its nose to alter the sounds.

Most bat sounds are too high for humans to hear. How high a sound is (its pitch) is measured by its frequency, in beats per second, or hertz (Hz).

Spear-nosed bats live in the southern United States and Central America. They use their complicated nose structures to modify the sounds they produce when echolocating. How these structures work is still a mystery.

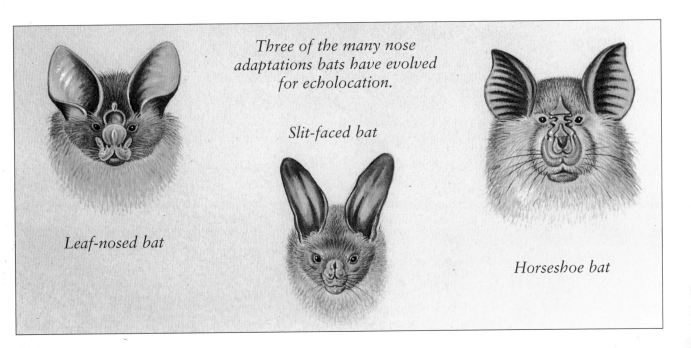

Three of the many nose adaptations bats have evolved for echolocation.

Slit-faced bat

Leaf-nosed bat

Horseshoe bat

Humans can hear sounds between 20 Hz and 20,000 Hz. Bats can hear between 100 Hz and 200,000 Hz (usually called 200 kilohertz, or 200 kHz). The sounds they make for echolocation are in the top part of this range. They are called ultrasonic sounds because they are beyond the normal human range of hearing. Young human ears work better than older ones so some children can hear bats calling, though adults cannot.

These sounds could not be studied until someone had found a way of hearing them. In the 1930s, 150 years after people found out that bats use their ears to "see," the right microphone was invented.

▼ *A whiskered bat turns its head in flight to listen to its surroundings. The leaves will give a constant image: The bat is searching for anything that moves.*

WATCHING BATS FLY

Finding out what bats can do in the dark was difficult at first, because the scientists could not see them. Eventually, they found that they could watch them in red light, which bats cannot see; to a bat a laboratory with only red lights is completely dark.

The results were amazing. They showed that bats could fly between thin threads hanging from the ceiling without touching them. If the threads were too close together, the bats turned away and flew in the other direction. They could avoid threads that were nearly invisible to humans.

Next, the scientists made a net from nylon strands no thicker than human hairs. The holes in the net were squares less than six inches (fifteen centimeters) across. They released some horseshoe bats, with a wingspan of nearly eighteen inches (forty-five

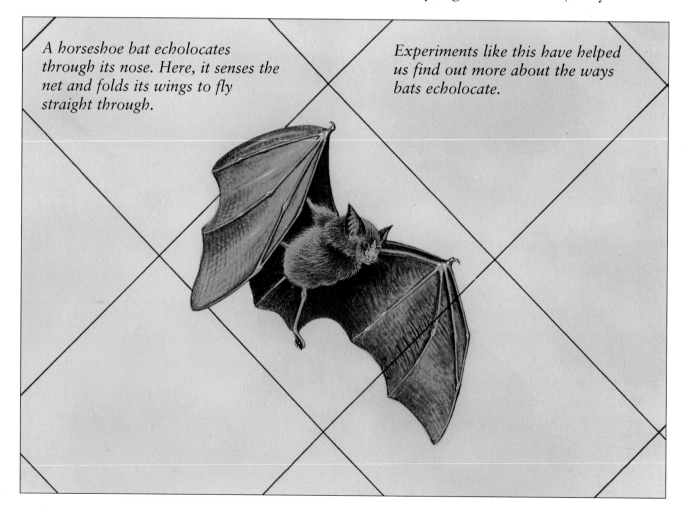

A horseshoe bat echolocates through its nose. Here, it senses the net and folds its wings to fly straight through.

Experiments like this have helped us find out more about the ways bats echolocate.

centimeters), and waited for them to become tangled in the net. The bats could "see" the net so clearly that they were able to fold their wings and dive between the strands without touching the sides.

In another experiment, scientists trained bats to catch tiny pieces of food thrown into the air. Later, they substituted things that were not food,

A greater horseshoe bat uses its wings to gather in a flying moth. Using echolocation, the bat can recognize not only the moth's movement, but also its shape and slightly fluffy texture, so that it knows it has found something worth catching.

though they were about the same size and shape. The bats could easily tell which was which and ignored the nonfood scraps. How did they do it?

LISTENING TO BATS

With a microphone that could pick up sounds humans cannot hear and a way of recording those sounds on paper, called a sonogram, scientists were ready to find out how echolocation works. Different species make sounds at slightly different pitches. In most species, each call falls quickly from a high note to a low one.

Scientists have invented a bat detector that picks up their sounds and converts them into clicks and warbles that we can hear.

High-flying bats that are traveling and not hunting make calls about one second apart. The echoes tell the bat how far away the ground is.

In contrast, bats flying among trees need more frequent information on their surroundings to avoid bumping into branches or tearing their wings on twigs. These bats make calls about ten times a second. The echoes from fluttering leaves come to them as a mixed-up sound, with many different frequencies. Among this jumble, the steadily beating wings of an insect or the slow movement of twigs stand out as separate notes

A serotine bat produces sounds from its open mouth. Its small bright eyes can see only the difference between light and darkness, but with its ears, it can "see" every leaf as it flies by.

The most complicated type of call is for hunting. It is very short, lasting about five-thousandths of a second. Hunting bats start out making five or six of these calls each second, but when they locate something they want to catch, the calls get faster. In the last moments of the hunt, they may be calling two hundred times a second.

UNDERSTANDING ECHOES

A bat learns a lot of detailed information from the echoes of its calls. It can judge distances because things that are near return an echo quicker and louder than things that are further away.

Different textures also produce different echoes. Hard, smooth things produce a sharp echo, while rough or furry things make a more muffled sound. The scientists who trained bats to catch scraps of food thrown into

A hunting bat calls then listens. Solid objects like the lamp post and the roof will give clear echoes because they don't move. Although the leaves move, the bat will be more interested in the moth flying freely in all directions.

the air and ignore other small things found that they can recognize shapes, too. For example, if the bats had learned that round balls were made of food and ovals were made of wood, they would let the ovals go. How they do this is hard to understand. They must pick out tiny differences in the echoes from different parts of the object.

Using echolocation, a fishing bulldog bat can detect the fin of a fish as it breaks the surface of the water by as little as 0.04 inches (1 millimeter). It trails its feet across the water to snatch up the fish with its sharp claws.

Collecting all this information and processing it in its large brain, the bat forms a picture of its surroundings and spots any moving objects that might be food.

THE HUNT

Bats hunting in the dusk look like leaves blowing in a gale, but every movement they make is completely under control. To catch insects in flight, a bat must react and turn in a split second. The amount of information going through its brain is hard to believe. Calling two hundred times a second, it must gather just as good a picture with its ears as we do with our eyes. When it is calling more slowly, it probably receives a jerky picture, perhaps like an old film.

A Bat Searches for Food

Slow calls explore . . .

We know that a bat looking for food makes five or six short, high-pitched calls each second, falling from high frequency to low in a continuous swoop. When one of these hunting calls produces the echo of something that sounds good to eat, the bat begins its approach-and-capture sequence. Sonograms of hunting bats show that it may take some of them as little as half a second from detecting prey to catching it.

A gray long-eared bat shows its teeth. Bats have three kinds of teeth. The canines, the long pointed teeth on either side at the front, grip struggling insects to stop them escaping. The incisors, the central front teeth, are too small to bite the victim into pieces, so bats have to chew whole insects with their molars, the wide rough teeth in their cheeks.

quicker calls locate . . .

and rapid calls pinpoint the prey.

Mexican free-tailed bats emerging at dusk from their roosting cave in Mason, Texas. By the time they return in the morning, each will have eaten thousands of mosquitoes and other small insects. Echolocation helps groups of flying bats avoid collisions. Each knows where those bats nearest are and in which direction they are flying.

The swooping calls come closer together to produce a clearer picture of its prey as the bat judges its size, shape, and texture and follows its movements. Often, a bat will scoop up an insect in its wings before grabbing it with its teeth. Bats eat small insects while they fly, but they may carry larger ones to a perch to devour more easily.

The calls made by bats are surprisingly loud. Measured from four inches (ten centimeters) away, a bat produces as much noise as a jet aircraft — fortunately at a frequency that humans cannot hear. Why don't these calls deafen the bats?

Having such sensitive ears, bats need a way of protecting themselves from their own incredibly loud calls.

▼ *A bat's inner ear is large and highly developed. In this x-ray, each circular object at the base of the skull is a cochlea, a coiled tube full of fluid with many nerve endings to receive the echoes of the bat's calls.*

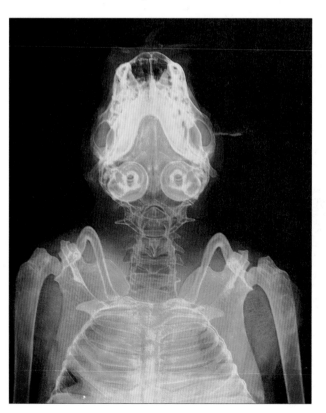

▲ *A long-eared bat dives toward a moth. Not all such attacks end in success. If the moth hears it and can reach cover, it might escape among the leaves.*

They do it with special muscles. All mammals have three small bones in their ear to transmit vibrations from the ear drum to the inner ear, where nerves pass messages to the brain. Bats have strong muscles attached to these bones so that they can switch off the ear while they are making a call and switch it on again in time to listen for an echo. It sounds simple, but it is astonishing to think that a bat can switch its ears on and off two hundred times per second when it is hunting.

Some bats make softer calls than others because the prey that they prefer can hear them coming and dodge out of the way. Thus, the battle between bats and moths is not a one-sided contest. Many moths have sound-detectors on the sides of their bodies, and some can produce sounds of their own to confuse hunting bats. Tiger moths taste bad, and they make clicking sounds to warn bats to leave them alone.

Bats that eat insects also need to drink regularly because their food is so dry. This Natterer's bat skims the surface of a pool to take up a mouthful of water.

A WORLD OF BATS

Nearly a quarter of all mammals are bats. There are more than 950 species, living everywhere except in the Arctic and the Antarctic and on the highest mountains. In the New World there are about 500 species.

Spear-nosed bats live from northern Argentina to the south-western United States. They eat fruit, plucking it from trees as they fly by and carrying it to a safe place to eat.

Two species of bulldog bats are found from Mexico to Argentina. The larger, fishing bulldog bat detects the ripples when a fish breaks the surface and snatches it up with the sharp claws on its long legs. The smaller species eats insects.

Vampire bats, found from Mexico to northern Argentina, have a fearsome reputation. They remove a small sliver of an animal's skin with their very

▲ *A vampire bat, about two inches (five centimeters) long, feeds on the nose of a sleeping pig. Vampire bats rarely attack humans, but if they do, they can transmit the virus that causes rabies.*

▶ *Tiny Honduran white bats spend the day roosting in a curled banana leaf.*

sharp front teeth and lap blood from the wound. A chemical in their saliva stops the blood from clotting while they drink.

Free-tailed bats feed on insects in warm areas. They form the largest colonies of any warm-blooded animal. The Mexican free-tail colony in Bracken Cave, Texas, may contain forty million bats.

In a shower of spray, a fringe-lipped bat in Panama seizes a frog. It locates its victims easily because it hears them calling all night long for mates. In one study, all the fringe-lipped bats each caught and ate a frog every ten minutes throughout the night.

Sheath-tailed bats live in warm countries all round the world. They include some of the smallest bats, with bodies little more than an inch (2.5 centimeters) long.

Common or vesper bats live everywhere that bats can live. They feed mostly on insects, but one species eats fish and others catch mice. They live in caves but many species also inhabit buildings.

▶ *Brown long-eared bats roost in the roofs of houses all over Europe, where it is against the law to interfere with them in any way.*

▼ *A short-nosed fruit bat feeds at a wild banana flower. The pollen grains on its head will be transferred to the next banana flower it visits.*

Horseshoe bats live in the Old World tropics, and in Europe and Japan. Their name comes from their horseshoe-shaped nose-leaf. Like vesper bats, they eat insects and often live in buildings.

In the Old World, the fruit-eating flying foxes, or fruit bats, include the world's largest bats, with a six-foot (nearly two-meter) wingspan. Their doglike faces give them their name. They fly by day, using their eyes. The only exception is the rousette bat, which uses a simple clicking system in the caves where it lives.

The rousette bat is the only fruit bat to use echolocation because it is the only one to sleep in caves, not in trees like the others. It is very crude compared to the true echolocators. Instead of calling with its voice box, the rousette bat makes a clicking sound with its tongue, listening for echoes from the cave walls. The calls are so low-pitched that even adult people can hear them as tinny clicks.

Once it has found its way outside, it uses its eyes to find trees with flowers, where it feeds on nectar and pollen.

A rousette bat in South Africa. Its simple ears and nose are signs that it is not specialized for echolocation. With its large eyes, it can see well in daylight.

OTHER ECHOLOCATORS

Bats are not the only animals to use echolocation. Dolphins, toothed whales, and some cave-living birds use a similar system of noises and listening. Seals, especially the deep-diving Weddell seal, make whistling and howling sounds underwater that may be a form of echolocation. Even little shrews use their high-pitched squeaks to find the entrance to their burrows after they have been out hunting.

To a pod of killer whales, the ocean is a world of sound. They communicate and navigate with whistles and clicks and hunt with high-frequency echolocation.

The killer whale's system starts out like that of a traveling bat, with low-frequency clicks about a second apart. These echo from rocks and the sea bottom — and other killer whales — but do not pick out anything smaller.

They occasionally make quicker bursts of sound as they search for food. When a group of whales finds some salmon, the clicks speed up to five hundred per second, sounding to human ears like a humming noise. The whales can interpret echoes from these clicks so accurately that they can tell a salmon from a cod more than a hundred feet (thirty meters) away.

▲ *Cave swiftlets in the Seychelle Islands survive in only one or two small colonies in caverns among boulders high in the hills.*

The cave swiftlet is the best-known echolocating bird because Asians often go to its caves to collect the nests for soup. Outside, the swiftlet twitters like other birds, but when it flies into the cave, its note changes to a series of twanging clicks.

25

HUMAN ECHOLOCATION

The sonar system, by which submarines find their way around under the sea, was invented during World War II, about fifty years ago. The idea came from studies of bats, though the human form of echolocation is still very simple.

A speaker in the submarine's hull makes a sharp ping that echoes from the seabed — or from another submarine — and a microphone feeds

the echo into the submarine's computer. The computer calculates the distance of the objects reflecting the pings. Like a bat's ears, the microphone can be moved around to listen in various directions, and the speaker, too, can be moved, like a bat's nose.

Ships also use sonar to track schools of fish and to measure the depth of water around them. Modern sonar can produce a detailed picture of the sea

bottom, but it is still crude compared to the accurate sound picture a bat needs to catch its prey.

Even without electronic help, humans can manage a form of echolocation. We can tell the difference between being out in the open and being indoors, even in complete darkness, because of the difference in the echoes that we hear. A small room sounds different from a barn, and a tiled bathroom sounds different from a living room with curtains and soft furniture to absorb the echoes.

In seabed sonar scanning, a transmitter fixed to the ship's hull sends out a sonar beam that can be moved up and down as well as sideways to locate wrecks and other items on the seabed. The photo below is an image produced by sonar.

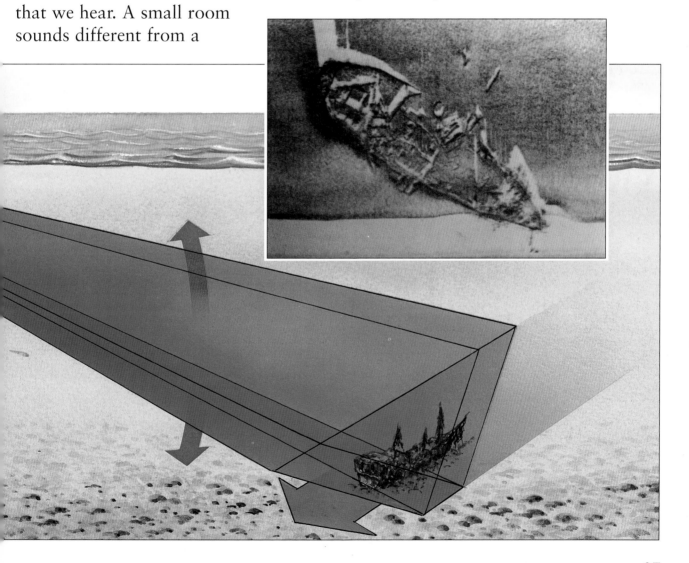

A little brown bat in the United States can catch and eat two mosquitoes every second. The forty million Mexican free-tailed bats from Bracken Cave in Texas eat more than five hundred tons of insects between them every evening when they go out to hunt. Not all insects are pests, but many damage crops or, like mosquitoes, carry diseases. Without bats, humans would have a far worse insect problem.

Many plants in the desert, like agave, produce nectar only at night, when there are no birds and few insects around to pollinate them. Cactus plants, too, open only in the dark. All these desert plants are pollinated at night by bats. Trees like the baobab in Africa and ironwood in Australia depend on bats if they are to produce seeds. Without bats, these plants, and the people and animals that need them, would have a serious pollination problem.

Rain forests are being cut down all over the world, even though most people realize how important it is to protect them. The bare ground that remains when the trees have gone — if it is left alone — will eventually grow more rain forest. But no trees will grow there until the smaller plants have started — and their seeds are carried by bats. Without bats, the world would have even worse problems with the loss of its rain forests.

At dusk, the millions of Mexican free-tailed bats leave Bracken Cave, Texas, watched by Merlin Tuttle (right), the world's leading bat expert. He has proved how valuable bats are as pollinators and seed distributors, as well as in controlling insect pests.

▲ *A lesser long-nosed bat feeds at an organ pipe cactus fruit. It will distribute the seeds some distance away in its droppings later in the night.*

▶ *The Australian ghost bat is the world's largest echolocating bat. It is also in danger of extinction because the forests where it hunts are being destroyed.*

Though bats are often seen as scary night creatures, all over the world, people need bats. Insect control, pollination, and forest repair — for these reasons and more we must take care of these fearless flyers.

GLOSSARY

clotting: sticking together and becoming solid.

colony: a group of animals, usually of one species, living together in the natural world.

crop: plants grown for food.

extinction: the state when no more members of an animal species exist.

mammal: a warm-blooded animal with a furry skin that feeds its young with milk.

muscles: bands of tissue that contract to produce movement.

navigate: to find and follow a route.

pests: animals that harm humans or things that humans need or value.

pollinate: to transfer pollen from one flower to another to produce seeds.

prey: animals that are hunted for food by other animals.

roosting: sleeping.

saliva: a substance produced by glands leading into the mouth. It helps digestion.

vertebrates: animals with backbones.

wingspan: the distance from one wingtip to the other when the wings are stretched out.

FURTHER READING

Bash, Barbara. *Shadows of Night: The Hidden World of the Little Brown Bat.* San Francisco: Sierra Club Books, 1993.

Green, Carl, and William R. Sanford. *The Little Brown Bat.* New York, Crestwood House, 1986.

Greenaway, Frank. *Amazing Bats.* New York: Alfred A. Knopf, 1991.

Halton, Cheryl M. *Those Amazing Bats.* New York: Dillon Press, 1991.

Johnson, Sylvia A. *Bats.* Minneapolis: Lerner Publications, 1985.

Lovett, Sarah. *Extremely Weird Bats.* Santa Fe, NM: John Muir Publications, 1991.

Pringle, Laurence. *Batman: Exploring the World of Bats.* New York: Charles Scribner's Sons, 1991.

Riley, Helen. *The Bat in the Cave.* Milwaukee, WI: Gareth Stevens, 1989.

Wexo, John B. *Flyers.* Mankato, MN: Creative Education, 1991.

INDEX

Numbers in *italic* indicate pictures